D1379606

North Dakota

Jim Ollhoff

Visit us at
www.abdopublishing.com

Published by ABDO Publishing Company, 8000 West 78th Street, Suite 310, Edina, Minnesota 55439 USA. Copyright ©2010 by Abdo Consulting Group, Inc. International copyrights reserved in all countries. No part of this book may be reproduced in any form without written permission from the publisher. The Checkerboard Library™ is a trademark and logo of ABDO Publishing Company.

Printed in the United States of America, North Mankato, Minnesota.
012010 102012

Editor: John Hamilton
Graphic Design: Sue Hamilton
Cover Illustration: Neil Klinepier
Cover Photo: iStock Photo

Manufactured with paper containing at least 10% post-consumer waste

Interior Photo Credits: Alamy, AP Images, Bobcat Company, Comstock, Corbis, C.W. Peale, Dakota Wizards, Edward S. Paxson, George Catlin, Getty, Granger Collection, Independence National Historical Park, iStock Photo, John Hamilton, Karl Bodmer, Library of Congress, Mile High Maps, Mountain High Maps, One Mile Up, Photo Researchers, State University of Montana Library, and Tim Kiser.

Statistics: State population statistics taken from 2008 U.S. Census Bureau estimates. City and town population statistics taken from July 1, 2007, U.S. Census Bureau estimates. Land and water area statistics taken from 2000 Census, U.S. Census Bureau.

Library of Congress Cataloging-in-Publication Data

Ollhoff, Jim, 1959-
  North Dakota / Jim Ollhoff.
      p. cm. -- (The United States)
  Includes index.
  ISBN 978-1-60453-669-0
  1. North Dakota--Juvenile literature. I. Title.

F636.3.O45 2010
978.4--dc22

                          2008052320

Table of Contents

Peace Garden State

North Dakota is a land of vast cattle ranches and grain farms. The state's grasslands are perfect for grazing. The flat land is also ideal for growing wheat.

For thousands of years, Native Americans made their home in present-day North Dakota. They hunted, fished, and grew crops. When Europeans first came, they traded goods with the Native Americans. North Dakota didn't have as much bitter warfare between Native Americans and Europeans as other states.

Because the land is flat, it's possible to see a very long way. The sky looks very large in North Dakota. It is a big state, but not very many people live there. This makes for wide-open spaces and lots of nature.

Wild horses run across grasslands in
Theodore Roosevelt National Park, North Dakota.

Quick Facts

Name: The word *Dakota* means "friend" in the language of the Native American Sioux nation.

State Capital: Bismarck, population 59,503

Date of Statehood: November 2, 1889 (39th state)

Population: 641,481 (48th-most populous state)

Area (Total Land and Water): 70,700 square miles (183,112 sq km), 19th-largest state

Largest City: Fargo, population 92,660

Nickname: Peace Garden State; Flickertail State; Roughrider State

Motto: Liberty and Union Now and Forever, One and Inseparable

State Bird: Western Meadowlark

State Flower: Wild Prairie Rose

State Tree: American Elm

State Song: "North Dakota Hymn"

Highest Point: White Butte, 3,506 feet (1,069 m)

Lowest Point: Red River, 750 feet (229 m)

Average July Temperature: Ranges from 67°F (19°C) in the northeast to 73°F (23°C) in the south

Record High Temperature: 121°F (49°C) in the city of Steele on July 6, 1936

Average January Temperature: Ranges from 3°F (-16°C) in the northeast to 14°F (-10°C) in the southwest

Record Low Temperature: -60°F (-51°C) in Parshall on February 15, 1936

Average Annual Precipitation: 14 inches (36 cm) to 22 inches (56 cm)

Number of U.S. Senators: 2

Number of U.S. Representatives: 1

U.S. Postal Service Abbreviation: ND

Geography

North Dakota spreads out over 70,700 square miles (183,112 sq km). It is the 19th-largest state. It borders Minnesota to the east. Montana is on the west side of the state. South Dakota is to the south. Canada is on the north border of the state.

North Dakota is in an area called the Great Plains. This part of the central United States is very flat. Most of North Dakota is flat, with some low, rolling hills. The elevation of the land rises toward the west.

On the western side of North Dakota is an area called the Badlands. Many thousands of years ago, some of the state was covered by glaciers. When the temperature got warmer, the glaciers melted. Rushing water from melting glaciers carved deeply into the rock, forming the Badlands.

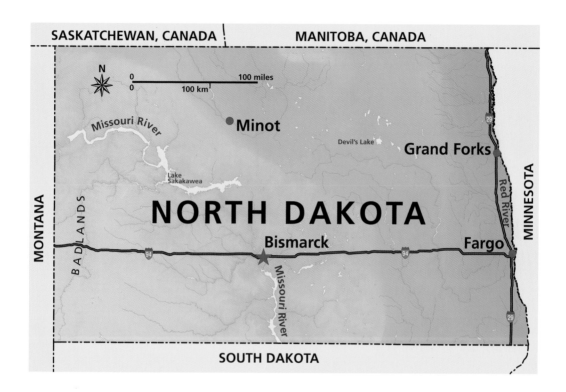

North Dakota's total land and water area is 70,700 square miles (183,112 sq km). It is the 19th-largest state. The state capital is Bismarck.

The Badlands have high cliffs and deep valleys. They also have steep, tall rocks called buttes. Theodore Roosevelt National Park is in the North Dakota Badlands.

North Dakota is rich in farmland and ranchland. Farmers grow wheat, rye, oats, and other crops. On ranches, people raise cattle and other animals. In the east, the Red River forms most of North Dakota's border with Minnesota. The Red River Valley has much fertile farmland.

The nation's third-largest non-natural lake is in North Dakota. It is called Lake Sakakawea. Engineers created the lake in 1956 for better flood control. The lake also provides hydroelectric power. It is named in honor of the Native American woman who traveled with Lewis and Clark in 1804-1806. The largest natural lake in the state is Devil's Lake.

The North Dakota Badlands.

Climate and Weather

   Large bodies of water create milder temperatures in the surrounding area. But North Dakota is far from any ocean or great lake. So, the state has extremes in temperature and weather.

   North Dakota has hot, dry summers. Temperatures often get into the high 80s degrees Fahrenheit (lower 30's C). Because the land is so flat, there is a lot of wind.

   The state also has very cold winters. Temperatures in January often sink below zero. Freezing winds called Alberta clippers whip down from the Arctic. Average snowfall can reach 38 inches (97 cm) or more. Melting snow can cause dangerous flooding in the spring. In 1997, floods in Grand Forks caused a lot of damage.

In April 1997, most of the people of Grand Forks had to leave when water from the Red River flooded nearly the entire town.

Plants and Animals

Most of North Dakota was once covered by many kinds of grasses. This type of land is called prairie. There are not many trees or forests. The grasses provide nesting for birds and other animals. The heavy layer of grass also keeps soil healthy. Today, much of North Dakota's prairie grass has been replaced by farms.

The grassy land was a good home for buffalo and antelope. Sadly, buffalo were hunted until they were almost extinct. Today, buffalo herds are protected in parks.

Buffalo live well on North Dakota's grasslands.

Some of North Dakota is wetland. A wetland is an area that holds water for a long time. A swamp is a good example of a wetland. Wetlands are important because they filter out pollution. Wetlands can also keep floods from happening as often. Many animals live in the wetlands, like beavers and muskrats.

North Dakota wetlands.

White-tailed deer are a common sight in North Dakota.

Red fox and coyotes are common in North Dakota. White-tailed deer, skunks, badgers, and prairie dogs also make their home in the state.

The most common fish in North Dakota waters include yellow perch, northern pike, and walleye. There are also bluegills, bullheads, and white suckers.

There are many birds and animals that are endangered. This means that only a few are left in North Dakota. These endangered animals include wolves, pumas, bobcats, bald eagles, and river otters. In fact, North Dakota has 64 protected wildlife refuges, which is more than any other state.

North Dakota's pumas are endangered.

Coyote

Badger

Gray Wolf

History

Native Americans have lived in North Dakota for thousands of years. Some of the big tribes were the Mandan, Hidatsa, Arikara, Sioux, and Chippewa.

French explorer La Vérendrye is the first known European to visit Native Americans in North Dakota.

These tribes farmed, hunted, and traded with each other. They also sometimes made war on each other.

In about 1738, a French explorer named La Vérendrye visited villages of the Mandan tribe. He was looking for a path to the Pacific Ocean. This is the first known contact between European people and Native Americans in North Dakota. La Vérendrye set up posts to trade with the Native Americans.

Mah-to-toh-pa, or Four Bears, of the Mandan tribe, painted by George Catlin in 1832.

The United States purchased a large area of land from France in 1803. This was called the Louisiana Purchase. This land would later be divided into many different states, including North Dakota.

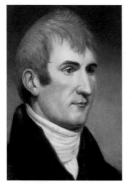

Meriwether Lewis and William Clark explored the West from 1804-1806.

In 1804, Meriwether Lewis and William Clark led an expedition that explored the West. They were sent by President Thomas Jefferson. In the winter of 1804-1805, they built a fort near the present-day city of Washburn. From there, Lewis and Clark traveled all the way to the Pacific Ocean. They came back through North Dakota on their way home, in 1806.

By the 1830s, many of the Native American people had died. They caught many diseases from the Europeans. The worst disease was smallpox. The Mandan tribe was almost wiped out by this sickness.

In 1861, the United States Congress organized the Dakota Territory. It included the modern-day states of North Dakota, South Dakota, Montana, and parts of Wyoming.

Fort Mandan, near today's Washburn, North Dakota, was built by the Lewis and Clark expedition in the winter of 1804-1805.

Railroads were built in the 1870s. This brought many settlers to the state. Farmers on big farms grew wheat. The grain was shipped on railroads to Minnesota, where it was made into flour.

Railroad construction in 1879. A Northern Pacific grading crew works in the Big Cut, Beaver Creek Valley, western North Dakota.

On November 2, 1889, both North and South Dakota were admitted to the United States. North Dakota became the 39th state.

New settlers started farms and ranches. Mines, brickworks, and flour mills sprang up. The railroads

North Dakota farmers break soil to begin planting in the 1900s.

provided many new jobs and created new towns.

North Dakota had a hard time in the 1920s and 1930s. Banks closed, farmers had no money, and businesses closed. Droughts made it hard for farmers to grow crops. The Great Depression hit the United States in 1929. Few people had money and many lost their jobs. The Great Depression hit North Dakota very hard.

World War II created a need for more food from places like North Dakota. Things got better in the state.

In the 1960s, the United States military built air bases in North Dakota. This brought many jobs to the state.

Did You Know?

- President Benjamin Harrison signed important laws on November 2, 1889. They made North Dakota and South Dakota the 39th and 40th states. Which became a state first? No one knows for sure. President Harrison kept it a secret. Historians say North Dakota came first only because it comes before South Dakota in the alphabet.

- Salem, North Dakota, is home to the world's largest Holstein cow. Salem Sue stands 38 feet tall (12 m) and weighs about 6 tons (5.4 m tons).

- Each year North Dakota ranchers raise enough beef cattle to make 113 million hamburgers. The state's farmers grow enough potatoes annually to make 207 million servings of French fries.

- Before he became the 26th president, Theodore Roosevelt came to North Dakota. He arrived in 1883 to hunt and establish cattle ranches. After he became president, Roosevelt said, "I never would have been president if it had not been for my experiences in North Dakota." Today, Theodore Roosevelt National Park is in the rugged Badlands of North Dakota.

Phil Jackson (1945–) is one of the most successful National Basketball Association coaches in history. Jackson played basketball at his high school in Williston, North Dakota, and for the University of North Dakota. Jackson played professional basketball for the New York Knicks and the New Jersey Nets. He began coaching in 1987 for the Chicago Bulls, who won six championships in nine seasons. He went on to coach the Los Angeles Lakers, and once again guided the team to many winning seasons. In 2009, Jackson won his tenth NBA championship title, more than any other head coach.

Dr. Anne Carlsen (1915–2002) was born without complete arms or legs, but still became a high school teacher. She earned her doctorate degree and worked for a school for children with disabilities in North Dakota from 1938-1981. The Anne Carlsen Center for Children in Jamestown, North Dakota, continues to help disabled children to be successful citizens.

Lawrence Welk (1903–1992) was born in Strasburg, North Dakota. Welk became a bandleader. He starred on a TV show for more than 30 years, starting in 1951. The show featured singers, dancers, and music. The *Lawrence Welk Show* was one of the most popular shows on television for many years.

Josh Duhamel (1972-) is a popular movie and television actor. Duhamel is most well known for his work in the movie *Transformers* and the television shows *Las Vegas* and *All My Children*. Duhamel was born in Minot, North Dakota, and attended Minot State University. In addition to acting, he was the official celebrity pace car driver for the 2009 Indianapolis 500 race.

Eric Sevareid (1912–1992) was born in Velva, North Dakota. He became a television journalist. He was famous for helping people understand the news, instead of simply reporting it. Sevareid covered World War II in Europe and Asia.

Carl Ben Eielson (1897–1929) was born in Hatton, North Dakota. He became a daring aviator and pilot in Alaska. He was the first person to fly across the Arctic Ocean, in April 1928. He flew many trips in Alaska. He died in an airplane crash while attempting to rescue people who were trapped on the ice.

Cities

Fargo is the largest city in North Dakota. Its population is 92,660. Fargo was formed in 1871. Steamboats on the Red River used the city as a stopping point. So, over the years, a city sprang up. Today, Fargo has four colleges, including North Dakota State University.

Hot-air balloons soar over the city of Fargo, North Dakota.

The capital of North Dakota, and the state's second-largest city, is **Bismarck**. It is located in the middle of the state. Its population is 59,503. The city was founded in 1872. Its original name was Edwinton. One year later, citizens changed the name to Bismarck, after German leader Otto von Bismarck. They were trying to attract German residents. Today, Bismarck has many museums and several colleges.

The capitol building in Bismarck.

NORTH DAKOTA CAPITOL

With more than 51,740 people, **Grand Forks** is the third-largest city in the state. It sits at the fork of the Red River and the Red Lake River, which is why it is named Grand Forks. The city is the home of the University of North Dakota. An important Air Force base is also in Grand Forks.

Minot is in the north-central part of the state. It became a town in 1886, when the railroads came through the area. The city was named after Henry

Minot in 1941.

Davis Minot, who was a friend of the railroad owner. Today, the city's population is 35,281. Minot State University and Minot Air Force Base provide many jobs for the people of the city.

Minot Air Force Base.

Transportation

There are 86,609 miles (139,384 km) of public roads in North Dakota. Of those, 572 miles (921 km) are interstate highways. The major interstate highways are I-29, going north and south, and I-94, which goes east and west. There are 4,521 road bridges in North Dakota.

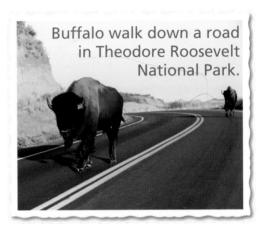

Buffalo walk down a road in Theodore Roosevelt National Park.

Railroads have been important in the state since the 1870s. In the 1880s, a rail line was built through North Dakota, from St. Paul, Minnesota, to Seattle, Washington. Railroads continue to be important today. There are more than 2,500 miles (4,023 km) of railroad track.

A North Dakota Air National Guard F-16 takes off from Hector International Airport in Fargo.

The busiest airports in North Dakota include Hector International Airport in Fargo, Bismarck Municipal Airport, Grand Forks International Airport, and Minot International Airport. There are almost 100 airports in the state, although most handle only very small planes.

Natural Resources

North Dakota farmers grow potatoes, wheat, rye, and oats. North Dakota is first in the nation in growing barley, sunflower, and flaxseed. They also raise beef cattle. The single most important crop for farmers is wheat. In fact, North Dakota farmers produce enough wheat each year to make 16 billion loaves of bread.

North Dakota has about 32,000 farms. Farms have increased in size over the last few decades. The average-sized farm today is about 1,241 acres (502 ha). Because there is more machinery, fewer people are needed to work on the farms.

In 1951, oil was discovered near Tioga, in the northwest corner of the state. North Dakota became a big producer of oil. The state also mines a small amount of lignite, also called brown coal.

A farmhouse stands in the middle of a North Dakota wheat field. Wheat is the single most important crop in the state.

Industry

Farming and ranching are the biggest industries in North Dakota. In addition, the Air Force bases in North

An oil drilling rig in the Badlands.

Dakota give jobs to many people. Manufacturing, mining of lignite, and oil production employ many people. Government jobs are also important.

Ten of the top 12 employers in North Dakota are in the health care field. These include hospitals and medical insurance companies. The universities in North Dakota are also big employers. Bobcat, an equipment manufacturer, is another top employer.

The Bobcat headquarters is in West Fargo.

The biggest source of income in North Dakota is agriculture, followed by mining of coal and natural gas. The third-biggest source of income is the growing tourism industry. North Dakota tourism sites are rich and varied. Tourists can admire the rugged beauty of the Badlands. People can see the International Peace Garden, located on the Canadian border near Dunseith, which is dedicated to peace in the world. Or,

The gardens and structures at the International Peace Garden in Dunseith, North Dakota.

tourists can go to Casselton and see the largest stack of empty oil cans in the world.

Sports

North Dakota has no major league sports teams. The Dakota Wizards are a minor league basketball team. Team members play in hopes of getting to play in the National Basketball Association (NBA). The Dakota Wizards have won championships among the minor league teams.

Many people in North Dakota follow college sports. The University of North Dakota and North Dakota State University have popular teams.

North Dakota hosts a walleye fishing tournament each year. There are also several rodeos in the state.

There are many outdoor activities for the people of North Dakota. There are state parks and wildlife refuges.

There are more than 1,300 campsites. Biking, hunting, horseback riding, and fishing are favorite pastimes. In winter, people enjoy snowmobiling, cross-country skiing, and ice fishing.

Mountain bikers enjoy a prairie path across North Dakota's Little Missouri National Grassland.

Entertainment

The city of Bismarck has North Dakota's largest zoo, the Dakota Zoo. It opened in 1961. Today, it has 125 species of birds and animals. The Chahinkapa Zoo, in Wahpeton, includes a hands-on petting zoo.

The North Dakota Museum of Art in Grand Forks has many exhibitions. The museum focuses on national and international art. It also has collections of modern Native American art.

The North Dakota Heritage Center in Bismarck is a place to study the past and learn more about the history of North Dakota.

There are many historic sites that preserve early forts. The Camp Hancock State Historic Site in Bismarck was once part of a military camp established in 1872. It was originally built to protect railroad workers.

In Dickinson, there is a dinosaur museum. There are dinosaur bones from all over the world at this museum.

There are plenty of small and local museums, festivals, and fairs. There's always something to do in North Dakota.

The Dakota Dinosaur Museum in Dickinson, North Dakota, has dinosaur bones from all over the world.

Timeline

9,500 BC—Paleo-Indian peoples live in the area. They hunt mammoths and giant bison.

1600—The Cheyenne, Mandan, and Hidatsa peoples live in the area. The Dakota-Sioux live throughout eastern and central North Dakota.

1610—Henry Hudson claims a large area of land, including North Dakota, for England.

1682—France claims all land around the Mississippi River, including North Dakota.

1738—French explorer La Vérendrye visits the Mandan villages. This is the first known contact between European people and Native Americans in North Dakota.

1803—The United States buys a huge area of North America from France. The Louisiana Purchase includes much of North Dakota.

1804—Lewis and Clark, with their group called the Corps of Discovery, enter North Dakota. They spend the winter at Fort Mandan.

1861—Dakota Territory is officially organized. Settlers arrive.

1889—North Dakota becomes the 39th state.

1978—President Carter changes North Dakota's Theodore Roosevelt National Memorial Park into Theodore Roosevelt National Park, protecting the land for all Americans.

2009—The Red River floods near Fargo, North Dakota. Thousands of sandbags are placed to hold back the water.

Glossary

Alberta Clippers—Quick-moving storms that bring high winds, snow, and very cold temperatures across the northern United States. These storms often seem to begin in the western Canadian province of Alberta.

Badlands—A desert-like area that has deep cliffs, steep rocks, and areas that have been washed away by water.

Great Depression—A time in the United States, beginning in 1929, when many people lost their jobs, and almost everyone lived on limited income.

Hidatsa—A Native American tribe that lived in North Dakota before the Europeans came. They were also called the Minnetaree.

Lewis and Clark Expedition—An exploration of the West, led by Meriwether Lewis and William Clark, from 1804-1806.

Louisiana Purchase—In 1803, the United States purchased the middle section of North America from the French. Most of North Dakota was part of the Louisiana Purchase.

Mandan—A Native American tribe that lived in North Dakota before the Europeans came. They lived in permanent villages along the Missouri River and two of its tributaries, the Knife and Heart Rivers.

Prairie—A grassy land with few trees.

Sioux—A Native American tribe that lived in North Dakota before the Europeans came. There are three major divisions among the Sioux: the Dakota, Lakota, and Yankton.

Smallpox—A terrible, often deadly, disease that wiped out many Native American villages.

Index